Gallery Books
Editor: Peter Fallon

THE GENTLE ISLAND

Brian Friel

THE
GENTLE
ISLAND

Gallery Books

This edition of
The Gentle Island
is first published
simultaneously in paperback
and in a clothbound edition
on 30 June 1993.

The Gallery Press
Loughcrew
Oldcastle
County Meath
Ireland

ISBN 1 85235 110 1 (*paperback*)
      1 85235 111 X (*clothbound*)

    The Gallery Press receives financial assistance from An Chomhairle Ealaíon / The Arts Council, Ireland, and acknowledges also the assistance of the Arts Council of Northern Ireland in the publication of this book.

Characters

MANUS SWEENEY
JOE, his son
PHILLY, his elder son
SARAH, Philly's wife
PETER QUINN
SHANE HARRISON
BOSCO
TOM
CON
ANNA ⎫
        ⎬ Sarah's parents
NEIL ⎭
MARY
PADDY
MARTIN

Time and place

The action takes place on the island of Inishkeen, off the
west coast of Co. Donegal.

Time — the present.

The Gentle Island was first produced at the Olympia Theatre, Dublin, on 30 November 1971, with the following cast:

MANUS SWEENEY	Liam Redmond
SARAH	Sheelagh Cullen
JOE SWEENEY	Eamonn Morrissey
TOM	Eamonn Draper
BOSCO	Niall O'Brien
ANNA	Virginia Cole
CON	Seamus Healy
PADDY	Joe Conway
MARTIN	David Herlihy
MARY	Maureen Toal
NEIL	Paul Farrell
PHILLY SWEENEY	Bosco Hogan
PETER QUINN	Edward Byrne
SHANE HARRISON	Shane Connaughton
Direction	Vincent Dowling

for David Hammond

ACT ONE

Scene One

About one-third of the stage area, the portion upstage right from the viewpoint of the audience, is occupied by the kitchen of MANUS SWEENEY's *cottage. The rest of the stage area is the street around the house. Against the gable wall are a currach, fishing nets, lobster-pots, farming equipment.*

There are two doors leading off the kitchen, one on each side of the fireplace. One leads to MANUS/JOE *bedroom, one to* SARAH/PHILLY *bedroom. There are no walls separating the kitchen area from the street.*

A morning in the month of June. The inhabitants of Inishkeen, an island off the west coast of County Donegal, are leaving for good — all except MANUS SWEENEY *and his family. Most of the islanders are already in the boats. The last few hurry past Sweeney's house on their way down to the harbour. They are dressed in their best clothes.*

When the play opens MANUS *is sitting in an airplane seat in the kitchen, his back to the audience, staring resolutely into the fire. He is in his sixties, well made, still enormously powerful even though the muscles are now muted with flesh.*

SARAH, *his daughter-in-law (Philly's wife), is sewing at the kitchen table. Occasionally she glances quickly out the window and down towards the harbour. She is dressed in men's boots, long skirt, coarse knitted jumper.*

Silence. Then JOE *rushes in from the left. He is carrying a spade — he has been splicing the handle. He is in his twenties. Like his father he has a big physique, but his strength is more brutal, not as precise, not as economical.*

JOE   Father! Father! Come here quick! Sarah! Sarah! You're missing it all! There's four in one boat and six in the other and they're trying to get aul' Nora Dan to change over but they can't get a budge out of her. (*Shouting*) Good on you, Nora! She's sitting there in the stern, Father, clutching the box of hens on her knee and she's not going to move for man or beast. By God, are they — ? My God, they're going to lift her, hens and all! Sarah, Father, come here 'till you see! Eamonn and Big Anthony have her by the arms — they're pulling at her — the boat's rocking — Jaysus, she's in the water! — no, no, only the hens. Oh Christ, she's going mad! She's caught Eamonn by the hair of the head and she's kicking the shins off Big Anthony. They're all pulling and tearing at her now. God, she's biting and spitting and butting and flinging! Father, come here 'till you see!

Two young men enter in a great hurry from up left. BOSCO *is carrying the mattress on his back.* TOM *has two huge cases.*

TOM Yes, Joe.

JOE Yes, men.

TOM Great hooley last night, wasn't it?

JOE Powerful. What the hell's the mattress for, Bosco?

BOSCO Get the knickers off, all you Glasgow women! The Inishkeen stallions is coming!

JOE Go on, you bastard you.

TOM No chance of him changing his mind?

JOE Who?

TOM Who d'you think? — Your aul' fella.

JOE For Christ's sake — no one left here but us — we own the whole island now.

BOSCO And welcome to it.

TOM I didn't see Philly at the do last night. Where was he?

BOSCO Where is he always?

JOE Started the salmon. Single-handed. He's not in yet.

BOSCO It's a buck like me Sarah should have got. Jaysus, I'd never rise out of the bed except to eat.

TOM Say goodbye to him, will you?

BOSCO And to Sarah.

JOE Right. Right. You'd better hurry.

TOM Is your father about, Joe?

BOSCO (*Calls*) So long, Manus!

JOE He's up the hill. He wouldn't hear you.

TOM Goodbye, Joe.

JOE Good luck, lads.

BOSCO Get them off! Get them off! The Donegal bulls is coming for you!

They go off down left.

JOE Bloody madmen. You should see them, Father; you'd think they were going to a bloody dance. Bloody madmen . . . Damnit the first boat's pulling out. She's lying very low in the water. Someone's standing up and waving — (*He waves back*) — it looks like Barney Pat — God, aul' Barney — (*Softly*) Good luck, aul' Barney. Damnit he's got his fists clenched above his head and he's shaking them. What the hell's he at?

Sound of drunken singing. CON *enters upstage left. He has a bottle of whiskey in his hand. He has been drinking for days and is almost inarticulate. He is being steered and prodded along by his daughter* ANNA. *When she appears* JOE *becomes embarrassed.*

Yes, Con. Yes, Anna.

ANNA Are we the last?

JOE Almost.

ANNA Here's the key to the door. Maybe you'd light an odd fire — you know, to keep the place aired.

JOE Surely.

ANNA Might as well have it cosy for the fieldmice.

CON (*Calls into house*) She's bringing me to a place called Kilburn, Manus.

JOE I'll write you every Sunday night, Anna. Sarah'll do it for me. She's smarter with the pen than me.

CON (*Calls*) In London.

ANNA (*To* CON) We'll miss the boat.

JOE And Philly'll post it every Monday when he goes out to the fish auction. I'll — I'll — I'll tell you all the news about here.

ANNA They'll be long letters.

CON (*Calls*) Goddamn you, Manus Sweeney, you won't always be as well set up as you are now.

ANNA Come on, Father, come on.

JOE Anna, I'll —

ANNA The boat's going to leave without us.

CON (*To* JOE) One bloody room in bloody Kilburn, son.

ANNA I'm going without you.

CON D'you think was the Flight of the Earls anything like this?

ANNA Come on! Come on! There's only one boat left.

CON bursts into song and plunges off.

CON 'My name is O'Donnell, the name of a king
And I come from Tirconnell whose beauty I sing.'

He goes off down left. ANNA, *afraid he'll fall, moves after him.*

JOE Anna, I will write to you, Anna.

ANNA You hadn't that much to say to me when I was here.

She goes off down left.

JOE Honest to God I will. Sarah will. (*Shouts*) Anna! Anna, I . . .

He breaks off suddenly and glances back in embarrass-ment at the kitchen.

Did you see Con, Father? Full as a bloody skin, the bastard. Jaysus, he hasn't sobered for nine days, that fella. Wants his head kicked in. That's what he wants. His bloody head kicked in.

Enter PADDY *and* MARTIN. PADDY *a strong, determined man in his late thirties, walking towards the harbour as if he were in a daze, looking neither left nor right. His son,* MARTIN, *aged about ten, acting very manly, trots beside him.*

MARTIN Yes, Joe.

JOE Yes, Martin. Look after yourself, boy. Good luck, Paddy.

PADDY hesitates, then goes on.

MARTIN Shake the aul' fella's hand for me, Joe.

JOE I'll do that, Paddy. I hope you have the best of luck over there. I hope you . . .

But PADDY *has gone, as has* MARTIN. JOE *looks after them.*

MARY Hold on! Hold on! We're coming! We're coming!

Enter up left MARY *and* NEIL — *Sarah's parents.* MARY *is a brisk, efficient woman. She has decided that by keeping talking this situation can best be handled.* NEIL *is smiling — and on the point of breaking down. He is in his bare feet and carries his shoes in his hand.*

(*Shouting towards harbour*) Hold on! Hold on! We're coming! We're coming!

On hearing her mother's voice, SARAH *comes out to the street.*

I'm at that fool of a father of yours for the past month to throw the dog into the tide but he has to leave it to the last minute. And then what happens? The rope breaks and the dog bites his hand and he falls into the water himself and destroys his Sunday shoes. (*To* JOE) He's bound to come about looking for food. Put a shot in him, will you, Joe?

JOE Right, Mary.

MARY (*To* SARAH) Now. I've left all the blankets and sheets on the kitchen table. Take what you want. Leave what you

15

want. There's a bag of meal up in the loft that'll do the hens and there's three sacks of seed potatoes inside the byre door. Where's Philly?

SARAH He's out at the salmon, Mother.

Pause.

MARY Thank God you got a sensible man — not like the fools I seen drinking themselves stupid last night. (*To* NEIL) Have you got the key? Mother of God, would you look at that! Put on your shoes, man!

NEIL They're —

MARY I know they're wet! But I'm not leading you into Manchester like an early Christian pilgrim!

NEIL *hands the key to* SARAH.

NEIL It was the dog. He thought I was going to drown him.

MARY And what were you trying to do? — Teach it to swim? My God, I married a fool. Come on. Move. Move. Say goodbye to Philly for us. And your father, Joe. We'll be back for the whole of July and August next year — or sooner, if needs be. (*Softly, to* SARAH) Any news to tell your sister beyond?

SARAH What sort of news?

MARY You're not throwing up your food or putting on weight, are you?

SARAH *turns aside.*

All in good time. Although when I was your length married I had Josephine talking and Christy crawling and Paddy in the cradle and I was six months gone with you and still that disciple was grinning at me like a sick sheep every time I bent over to put a turf on the fire. Lazy men are a constant burden to their wives. Thank your God you got an active one. By the time I get back you'll have your hands full. I left the cradle in the room down. Are we right? Goodbye, Joe.

JOE Goodbye, Mary. Good luck. Goodbye, Neil.

MARY Goodbye, *a thaisce*, see you next summer. Maybe
before — if I'm needed.

NEIL shakes his daughter's hand formally.

NEIL They'll be dry before I get to Derry.

Suddenly he throws his arms around her. They embrace.

SARAH Father . . . Father . . .
NEIL If you were coming too it'd be nothing, nothing at all.
MARY Lookat — you're holding them all up. Mother of God,
now the fool's going to cry!
SARAH I'll go down to the harbour with —
MARY You'll do no such thing. We're away! We're off! Send
for me if you want me. I can be back in a day. Come on!
Come on!

*She catches NEIL's arm and takes him with her off down
left. SARAH goes into the kitchen. JOE moves downstage.
Now MANUS rises slowly from his seat, comes to the
door, comes out on to the street. His left arm is missing.
The empty sleeve is tucked into the pocket of his jacket.
JOE glances back and sees his father. They stand silently
looking down at the harbour.*

JOE That's everybody. That's the last of them.

Pause.

Look at Bosco sitting up on top of his mattress. Playing
the aul' mouth organ . . . if you could hear him.

Pause.

Whatever wind there is is with them.

Pause.

MANUS When Philly gets back, tell him I'm away over to the

meadow to look at the sheep. I might shift them up to the far hill. The grazing on it might be better.

JOE You're king of the whole island now, Father. King of the whole bloody island.

MANUS The well needs to be cleaned out. If this weather keeps up we'll have to carry to the cattle.

JOE There'll always be bloody cattle.

MANUS I'll not be long.

JOE King of Inishkeen, King of nothing.

MANUS We haven't much. But we have enough.

JOE They don't think so.

MANUS They're doing a wrong thing.

JOE They're doing what they want to do.

MANUS This is where they belong.

JOE There was a vote taken.

MANUS They'll regret it.

JOE So they'll be back tomorrow — is that what you're saying? You're saying they'll be back tomorrow, next week, the week after? Is that what you're saying?

MANUS No.

JOE Damned right they won't. There should never have been anyone here in the first place.

MANUS Fifty years ago there were two hundred people on this island; our own school, our own church, our own doctor. No one ever wanted.

JOE Scrabbing a mouthful of spuds from the sand — d'you call that living?

MANUS And by God there'll be life here again.

JOE When? When they all come flocking back?

MANUS You could take up on them in that currach if you want to.

Pause.

JOE You — you — you haven't even the guts to bid them goodbye.

MANUS They belong here and they'll never belong anywhere else! Never! D'you know where they're going to? I do. I know. To back rooms in the back streets of London and Manchester and Glasgow. I've lived in them. I know. And that's where they'll die, long before their time — Eamonn and Con and Big Anthony and Nora Dan that never had a coat on her back until this day. And cocky Bosco with his mouth organ — this day week if he's lucky he'll be another Irish Paddy slaving his guts out in a tunnel all day and crawling home to a bothy at night with his hands two sizes and his head throbbing and his arms and legs trembling all night with exhaustion. That's what they voted for. And if that's what you want, it's there for the taking.

JOE goes off left with his broken spade. MANUS goes into the kitchen.

Sarah, where's my stick?

She hands it to him.

Guts! Talking to me about guts!

SARAH He's not much more than a boy. Couldn't you see he was going to cry?

MANUS What would he cry for?

SARAH For himself. For Anna.

MANUS Takes no guts to run away.

SARAH You're the man would know that.

MANUS You're turning into a sour woman.

SARAH It would be a comfort to him to know you did your share of running away, wouldn't it?

MANUS And a sour woman never made a home.

She goes into her bedroom. He goes out to the street. PHILLY enters right. He is wearing thighboots and carries an outboard engine across his shoulder. Unlike his father and his brother he is lightly built. And unlike all the other islanders, he talks quietly.

Well? How was it?

PHILLY Alright.

MANUS There was too little wind.

PHILLY There was enough.

MANUS Where did you go?

PHILLY North-east of the Stags.

MANUS The moon was bright.

PHILLY At times.

MANUS And that aul' net — you could put your head through it in places.

PHILLY It'll do.

MANUS Was it no good at all?

PHILLY They're down at the slip. I'll need a hand. Is Joe about?

MANUS (*Roars*) Joe! How many?

PHILLY A hundred and thirty.

MANUS Salmon?

PHILLY I would have shot again but she (*outboard*) started missing.

MANUS You're taking a hand at me!

PHILLY Nothing under five pounds.

MANUS God, Philly man, you're a prince! Joe! Sarah! They haven't come like that, sir, since I was a boy. And how did you haul them by yourself?

JOE *enters left.*

A hundred and thirty he got! One shot! And not a fish under five pounds!

JOE How many?

PHILLY They were that thick in the water you could have walked on them.

MANUS Twelve dozen — damn near. Twelve dozen on his first night. And him alone. We never began a season like that before. Never. Not even in the old days.

JOE How did you haul them?

MANUS He hauled them, boy! He hauled them!

JOE One shot?

MANUS With a bad net!

JOE Christ, Philly, that's fierce altogether. Good on you, man.

PHILLY They were in it. Anyone could have lifted them.

MANUS A mouthful of spuds from the sand, eh? And I told them, too. But they wouldn't listen to me. Rocks, dead, barren, they said. And their hearth-fires aren't right dead when Philly proves me right and proves them liars.

PHILLY Are they gone?

MANUS And all our bad luck go with them. We'll manage better without them. Fetch the barrow, Joe, and we'll bring home the first harvest.

He goes off right. PHILLY *takes the plug out of the outboard and cleans it carefully with a rag.*

JOE Jaysus, you made great work all the same. I'll go with you the night, Philly. Alright?

PHILLY Right.

JOE I'm not as awkward in a boat as he says.

PHILLY Him! He's a blether.

JOE Wasn't much blether from him last night. Felt a pity for the aul' bastard sitting in there by the fire, talking about the old days and about Mother and all.

PHILLY Mouth. I couldn't listen to him.

JOE He was telling me a good one about the first night he arrived in the States. He said when he got off the boat this wee Chinaman ran up to him and threw his arms about him and started shouting, 'Nephew! Nephew! Welcome, nephew, welcome!' And Father, Jaysus, he thought, maybe for all he knew this was the man Auntie Kate had married out there and she'd sent him to meet him, and Father he said, 'Thank you very much, Uncle Barney!' Jaysus!

PHILLY What did he say about Mother?

JOE She had long fair hair. I never knew that, Philly, did you? And I says to him sure her name was Rosie Dubh. And he said that was just a family name; but she was fair, he said. And his job was to plait it every night before she went to bed. And you should have seen his face when he was telling me.

PHILLY With one hand?

JOE One hand what?

PHILLY How did he plait it with one hand?

JOE Be God I never thought of that. With his mouth — that's it — with his mouth, too.

PHILLY Did he not go up to the do in Big Anthony's?

JOE No, he couldn't face it.

PHILLY Was it any good?

JOE I didn't go up until he went to bed.

PHILLY More fool you.

JOE And by that time all the aul' ones were stupid drunk and the young ones were going wild. About two in the morning Bosco and the boys built a haystack in the middle of the kitchen floor and then began wrestling on top of it.

PHILLY Eejits.

JOE And when they got tired of that they tied two cats together and went chasing after them through the house, throwing hot water over them.

PHILLY A hard man, Bosco.

JOE Bloody savage. This day week if he's lucky he'll be just another Paddy slaving his guts out in a tunnel in Scotland. That'll knock some of the bully out of him.

PHILLY You'd think you'd been there.

JOE Is Glasgow nice, Philly?

PHILLY Alright. What I saw of it.

JOE I'd like to see Glasgow. I'd like to see London. Jaysus, I'll be lucky if I ever see Dublin. (*Looking around the island*) It's like a Sunday when they're all out at Mass. Only the doors are shut and there's no smoke from the chimneys. (*Pause*) He says he's leaving me the lower fields and whatever beasts he has — if I'm here when he dies.

PHILLY With a ranch like that you'll be a gentleman farmer.

JOE Funny listening to him saying it all the same. And he's leaving you and Sarah the upper fields and the bog and the two boats and any other stuff there is about the place.

PHILLY That's big of him — I made the boats myself.

JOE And the house, too, for this is where he wants his grandchildren reared.

PHILLY He's waiting for the wheelbarrow.

JOE Be God I forgot.

He goes towards right, stops, takes ANNA's *key from his pocket and holds it up.*

Anna left me the key of her house. To light the odd fire in it. To have it nice for the fieldmice.

He looks at the key, then at PHILLY. *Then he pockets the key and goes off quickly.*
   PHILLY *takes off the big boots and goes into the house. He fills a basin with water and is washing when* SARAH *comes in from the bedroom.*

SARAH   You're back.
PHILLY   Aye.
SARAH   Tired?
PHILLY   A bit.
SARAH   D'you want something to eat?
PHILLY   I'll have a sleep first.

   Pause.

SARAH   How was the salmon?
PHILLY   Good.
SARAH   That'll please your father.
PHILLY   How are you?
SARAH   They're all away.
PHILLY   So. (*Pause*) How did the father and mother go off?
SARAH   She talked a lot.
PHILLY   I thought I would have been back in time but the tide didn't favour me.
SARAH   She left us blankets and meal and stuff. And a cradle if you don't mind.
PHILLY   What sort of form was he in?
SARAH   She sent him out to drown the dog this morning and he came back and said the rope broke. Couldn't even make up a good lie, the fool. And whatever messing he was at, he got his good shoes wet, and there he was, standing on the street in his bare feet and him going off to England and the wet socks sticking out of his pocket and not a sensible word out of his head and she says they'll be back next summer for two full months or sooner she says any time at all she's needed she says . . .

She almost cries but recovers. He watches her closely but makes no move towards her; she goes on almost formally, choosing her words with care.

Philly, I don't want to stay here. I want to go with them; not with my father and mother, but with all of them and with you, all of us together. I'll go out of my head with loneliness, I know I will.

PHILLY Easy.

SARAH It's nothing against your father or Joe. But the loneliness, Philly, the loneliness — I won't be able to thole it, Philly, I know I won't.

PHILLY You'll be alright.

SARAH We belong with the others. We should be with them.

PHILLY But they won't be together. As soon as they get to Derry they'll split up and they'll never see each other again. And when tonight comes there won't be a man of them that isn't wishing he was back here. D'you think your father's ever going to be content over there?

She shakes her head.

Or Con? Or Big Anthony? Or Nora Dan?

SARAH Because they're too old to change. But we're not.

PHILLY You know my plan. Stick it out until the end of the summer. I'll have made the most of £200 then. Then we'll pack up and off and bugger the lot.

SARAH That's what you said last year.

PHILLY I made nothing last year on account of the storms.

SARAH Your father'll never shift.

PHILLY He'll have his choice.

SARAH And you wouldn't leave him behind. You couldn't leave him alone.

PHILLY He'll have Joe, won't he? And when Joe gets sense and clears out he can talk his big talk to the rabbits for all I care.

SARAH And you wouldn't leave the sea.

PHILLY 'When Philly's on a boat he needs neither man nor food' — that's the way he rants.

SARAH Is he wrong?

24

PHILLY Any hard cash that comes into this house comes from the sea, not from his footering about the scraps of fields. And as long as I make money from it I'll fish it.

SARAH Maybe if you spent less time on it we might be better off.

PHILLY Farming? Here?

SARAH You and me.

Pause.

PHILLY I'm tired.

SARAH You're always tired when you're at home.

PHILLY I was up all night, woman. When you and the rest of them were away drinking and dancing I was working.

SARAH So you were.

He looks at her, uncertain what she means. He opens his mouth to say something more, decides against it, goes into the bedroom. She takes an empty bucket and goes off right.

PETER enters left. A plump, balding, middle-aged man. He is slightly out of breath from the climb up the hill. He is joined by SHANE, twenty years younger, peeling an orange. Both men are dressed in summer slacks and open shirts.

PETER My God, it's heavenly. Look, Shane, everywhere you turn, look at the view; you can see for a hundred miles. And the clarity. Look — there's the river where we camped the night before last and the lake where the lorry picked us up and the old railway station and the plantation where the men were cutting the spruce. And the sea, Shane, look at the sea. And there's not a sound — listen — not a sound. My God, this is heaven.

SHANE has been examining a stick he has picked up. He whispers nervously to PETER.

SHANE Apache.

PETER What?

SHANE Five-pointed star and the rising sun. Shhhh.

He grips PETER's *elbow and gives two low whistles.*

You think that's the cleft-palate whippoorwill?

He shakes his head slowly.

PETER Shane, let's forget about trying to make Galway. Let's
spend the last few days here. What do you say?
SHANE Has it a name?
PETER Inishkeen.
SHANE Apache name. Means scalping island.
PETER We'll put the tent up on that meadow down there —
no, on that green above the beach.
SHANE And sell pop to the kiddies.
PETER And for the rest of the holiday we'll just eat and sleep
and sunbathe and laze about. What about that? Maybe
we'll stay for a month — two months — maybe we'll
never leave! What do you say? Do you agree?

SHANE *is prowling about with exaggerated stealth.*

For the last few days we have then. I don't really want
to go to Galway. I'd rather stay here. I'm tired of hitch-
ing lifts and moving all the time. What about you? Will
you, Shane?
SHANE Sinister.
PETER I want to.
SHANE Too quiet.
PETER Please.
SHANE What are the facts, Sergeant? A dozen furnished
houses, all recently occupied. Crops in the fields. Some
cattle. But no people. Now. There is no evidence of a
hurried evacuation, so we can rule out plagues and
fiery dragons. And yet the atmosphere reminds me of
. . . Got it! Germany — Lower Saxony — 1940 —
parachuted in to join the Resistance. Saw this column
of Hitler Youth marching along country road leading
to mountain. Chap in strange uniform up front playing

recorder. Young people all laughing and singing. They reach the mountain. A door opens. They all march through. Disappear. Door shuts. Then silence. Not a sound. Just like here.

PETER   Shane, please be sensible, will you?

SHANE   Hamelin. That's the name of the place. Hamelin.

PETER   Stop fooling for a second.

SHANE   Why?

PETER   The boat's coming back for us. I want a decision made.

SHANE   You're wearing your *sincere* look.

PETER   Do we stay here or do you want to stick to the original plan and head for Galway?

SHANE   (*Sings*) 'And watch the sun go down on . . . '

PETER   Which is it to be?

SHANE   I've forgotten the question.

PETER   Stay here or head on.

SHANE   A choice.

PETER   Whatever you want.

SHANE   Yes.

    Pause.

PETER   Well?

SHANE   I hate choices, Peter.

PETER   I want to stay. What do you want to do?

SHANE   In the circumstances, M'Lord, I'm torn between emotion and intellect, between the old heart and the old head, and the trouble is —

PETER   The trouble is you've damn little of either. Okay. Fine. Right. We'll go. That's settled. Let's get away.

SHANE   Here!

PETER   Of course had I said I wanted to keep on the move, then wild horses wouldn't drag you away. But just because I said the damn place was pretty and that we could have a peaceful few days here, oh then Master Shane assumes his clown's costume and indulges in his juvenile jokes — the great protection. Fine, fine, fine, we'll go. We'll keep moving, talking, laughing, providing vast entertainment for every damn lorry driver that picks us up. What a jolly young man he is!

SHANE You're perspiring.
PETER Isn't it about time you dropped that façade of yours?

> SARAH *enters right carrying a bucket of water. They are
> not aware of her until she speaks.*

SARAH Good day to you.
PETER Oh — hello — good day.
SHANE (*To* PETER) Hiawatha.
SARAH How did youse get in?

> *They stare at her.*

How did youse get in to the island?
PETER A young man took us out — in — in his motor-boat, a
young man called Doherty from the mainland. He's to
come back for us within an hour. (*Pause*) We thought
all the houses were empty. (*Pause*) A very lovely place
you have here. (*Pause*) I hope — I hope — we're not
trespassing?
SARAH Are youse Yanks?
SHANE (*To* PETER) Christ!
PETER No, no, we're from Dublin.
SARAH Are youse touring about?
PETER Making our way down along the coast. Hitch-hiking.
SARAH There's nothing to see here.
PETER We visited four other islands further north. And then
we saw this one on the map. And this one's the fifth.
Inishkeen — what does the Irish name mean?
SARAH 'The gentle island'.
PETER Lovely — the gentle island. Beautiful name, Shane,
isn't it?
SARAH There's nothing here then.
PETER Perhaps you're used to it.
SARAH Were youse ever on the Isle of Man?
PETER No.
SARAH I was there. Six summers ago. I was a chambermaid in
the Arcadia Hotel in Douglas. It was great.
PETER Quite a change from here.
SARAH We worked from seven in the morning 'till ten at night

28

and we got every Sunday off and a half-day every second Thursday. And every night when the house-keeper went to bed, we slipped down the fire-escape and went to a dance. It was great.

PETER Every night? Weren't you exhausted?

SARAH In the eight weeks I was in Douglas I was at fifty-one dances. I wore out three pair of shoes. I never had a time like it.

PETER Why didn't you go back again?

SARAH You would like it.

PETER I prefer a less hectic holiday at my time —

SARAH Him. (*Shane*)

PETER Oh I thought you meant —

SARAH It's all young ones. He would have crack. What's your name?

PETER Peter Quinn. Shane Harrison.

SARAH What do you work at?

PETER We're teachers. Shane teaches engineering. I'm a music teacher.

SARAH You wouldn't be overworked here. Does he (*Shane*) say nothing?

PETER *turns to him.*

PETER Shane?

SHANE (*Accented English*) Eet ees most gratifying to our persons to be on thee Gentle Island.

SARAH What's he saying?

PETER Nonsense as usual. Pay no attention to him.

Enter MANUS *right.*

MANUS *Caide mar tá sibh? Tá fáilte romhaibh.*

PETER Good day.

MANUS How do you do, gentlemen?

PETER We're well.

MANUS Having a look over our island?

PETER Very briefly, I'm afraid. There's a boat coming back for us.

MANUS You've been down at the harbour and the beach?

PETER Yes, that's where we arrived.

MANUS And have you seen the cliffs on the east side?

PETER I'm afraid this is as far as we've got.

MANUS Oh you must see the cliffs — and the caves. No one leaves Inishkeen without seeing them. Come in and have a rest and then I'll show you where to go. You've come to a very beautiful place, gentlemen.

PETER I can see that.

MANUS What boat took you in?

SARAH Red Doherty. Said he'd be back for them in an hour.

MANUS Hah! You'll be lucky if he remembers you next month. Come in. Come in. I could do with a cup of tea myself.

PETER No, we can't trouble you with —

MANUS What trouble is there in making a cup of tea?

JOE enters right.

And it's seldom enough we have company. This is my son, Joe. And I'm Manus Sweeney. I'm the — hah! — I'm the king of Inishkeen.

The men shake hands.

Tea, woman. Come in — come in — it's a tight climb up that hill.

All enter kitchen except SHANE and SARAH.

PETER (*To* JOE) I see you've been out fishing.

JOE I wasn't. My brother Philly was. Last night.

MANUS And he got fifteen dozen salmon, sir. Single-handed. You'll have to meet Philly. The best fisherman on this coast. And Joe here's our farmer. And I'm the — what's the word for it? — I'm the coordinator. That's it. We're a self-contained community here.

SARAH Are you coming, engineer?

SHANE Why not?

SARAH No one going to eat you.

PETER That's an unusual chair.

Aware that SHANE *and* SARAH *are not in the kitchen he calls out to* SHANE.

Shane, come and see this chair.

SHANE *and* SARAH *enter.*

MANUS That's a comfortable chair. Sit down on it. I'll tell you about that chair. It came out of a German airplane that crashed into the side of this hill.

PETER (*Sitting*) Lovely.

JOE It was flung out in the explosion and the pilot was still in it.

MANUS And not a mark on him. Isn't that strange, sir? Not a scratch. We buried him in the old cemetery alongside the British sailors that were washed in.

PETER This was during the war years?

MANUS Rough times, gentlemen. We couldn't go away to work and there was no money coming in. Only we're a tough people there wouldn't be a trace of us now.

PETER Were you in the war yourself?

MANUS This? (*Arm*) No, I lost it in a mine in Butte, Montana. But that's another story.

JOE That clock came off a Dutch freighter that broke up on the Stags; and that table came off a submarine; and those lamps came off a British tanker; and these binoculars came off a French mine-sweeper. My father used to sit up all night waiting for the wreckage. All the men did. And they got bales of rubber and butter and tins of cigarettes and timber and whiskey and whatnot. Tell them about the night the Norwegian lifeboat floundered below the cliffs, Father, when the men were screaming and the —

MANUS The gentlemen'll think we're a race of scavengers. They were bad times. We had to live.

PHILLY *enters from bedroom.*

The fisherman himself!

PETER Your father tells me you got a big catch last night.

31

PHILLY It was alright.

MANUS (*To* PHILLY) Red Doherty brought them in. Told them he'd be back for them in an hour!

PETER We almost had an accident, too — didn't we? He was talking so much that he wasn't watching where he was going.

MANUS Red Doherty alright!

PETER And the next thing we brushed against a huge rock just off the harbour there.

JOE Them's the Monks.

PETER The what?

MANUS There's three rocks in it, two big ones and a wee one. We call them the Monks. There's a name for every stone about here, sir, and a story, too.

JOE Tell them about the Monks, Father.

MANUS I will not then. Night's the time for stories.

PETER What's the story?

MANUS It's a long one. I'll give it to you some other time.

PETER Is it a local legend?

JOE Go on and tell them. Go on.

PETER Do, please.

MANUS Some night I'll tell you. No man can tell a story right in the middle of the day.

JOE There used to be a monastery here hundreds of years ago — the ruins are still up there on our land; and the old monk in charge of it was' very stern and very powerful.

MANUS He'll only destroy it.

JOE And one summer his niece came to visit him.

PHILLY So beautiful was she that the fish came up from the sea and the birds down from the trees to watch her walk along the roads.

Pause. Everyone looks at PHILLY.

Isn't that the way it goes?

MANUS He has it.

JOE Jaysus we all know it! And two of the young monks fell for her and wanted to go away with her but she couldn't choose between them so she took the two of them off in a currach with her one black night. And the old monk seen them skiting off and he turned the three of them into three rocks below.

MANUS He's ruined it.

JOE But they knew if they could ever reach the mainland they'd be free from under his curse. So every night when it gets dark them three rocks begin creeping away from the island. But daylight always nabs them before they make the shore and back they have to come.

MANUS Now you've told it. And that's the Monks.

PETER It's a good story, Joe.

JOE I can't put a right skin on it though.

MANUS Anyhow you're here, gentlemen, despite the Monks.

PETER And Red Doherty.

MANUS Will you remain for a while?

PETER Just before you came along we were talking about staying here for three or four days — we have a tent and stuff down at the harbour — that's if you'd have no objection.

MANUS Stay. Surely stay. Put your tent anywhere you want. You're welcome. And there's milk and vegetables for the taking. All you need.

PETER We hadn't quite made up our mind.

JOE When the weather's good strangers all say it's nice here.

PETER (*To* SHANE) What about it?

JOE They could use Anna's house, Father. She wouldn't mind.

SARAH She didn't say it was for letting.

MANUS Your friend's a quiet man. What's he for doing?

PETER We'll stay, Shane. Please.

Pause.

SHANE Why not? Okay. Sure. We'll stay. We'll stay — why not?

Quick blackout.

ACT ONE

Scene Two

A few days later. Forenoon. Brilliant sunshine. SARAH *is setting the kitchen table. She is more attractively dressed and sings as she works.* SHANE *is out on the street. An ancient gramophone is sitting on an upturned creel and he is working at it.*

SHANE   Is there a pair of pliers in there, Sarah?

> *She does not hear him. He goes to the door and as soon as she sees him he acts an old black Southern slave.*

You got pliers about here, Missy Sarah Ma'am?
SARAH   What are you saying, you eejit you?
SHANE   Ah's lookin' foh pliers, Ma'am.

> *She gives him pliers from the large press.*

SARAH   Is that what you want?
SHANE   Bless you, li'l lady. Ole Joshua he sure fix you' music box real good now. Bl-ess you.

> *He shuffles off, humming.*

Ba-ba-be-do-be-da-boo-boo-boo-boo-boo-boo-dah.

> *She laughs at him and follows him to the door.*

SARAH   You made a good job of the radio, engineer. It's going stronger now than when it was bought.

> *He bows gallantly.*

These nights when Philly's out fishing, I lie in bed listening to it 'till almost daybreak. Sometimes I do listen to the music and sometimes to people talking in strange tongues and wonder what it is they do be talking about.

She comes out to the street.

I must call the men for the dinner.

She does not move.

You're a funny one, too.

SHANE I'm hilarious.

SARAH You're like the ones on the radio: half the time I don't know what you be talking about.

SHANE His ideas are trivial; pay little attention to what he says. But watch his hands — that's where his genius lies. He could open the vaults of the Bank of England with a gimlet. He could make a computer with a handful of tacks. But give him a hairpin, and with a hairpin he could create an electronic brain that would solve the problems of the world.

SARAH What age are you?

SHANE What age am I? 'You are old, Father William, the young man said, / And your hair has become very white; / And yet you increasingly stand on your head . . . ' Thirty-two.

SARAH Are your father and mother alive?

SHANE Father's a drummer in a beer-cellar in Hamburg called The Vicarage; and Mother's in Lapland. Every Christmas she's principal boy in the Lap National Pantomime. Last year they did Humpty Dumpty. They flew Father over to play the glockenspiel. No. I'm boasting again. I never knew either of them.

SARAH Have you any brothers?

SHANE Not that I know of.

SARAH Sisters?

SHANE No.

SARAH Were you born in Dublin?

SHANE   So they tell me.

SARAH   Have you got a house?

SHANE   No.

SARAH   Where do you live?

SHANE   A flat.

SARAH   In the town?

SHANE   In the town.

SARAH   Who cooks your food?

SHANE   I live on pieces of string and rusted hairclips.

SARAH   Have you any other friends besides Peter?

SHANE   Millions.

SARAH   Do you know him for long?

SHANE   Centuries.

SARAH   How long?

SHANE   He taught me.

SARAH   Peter?

SHANE   The same.

SARAH   He taught *you*?

SHANE   Correct.

SARAH   That's funny. What age is he?

SHANE   Seventeen or eighteen.

SARAH   He's sixty if he's a day! And he taught you!

SHANE stops working at the gramophone.

SHANE   Yes. I was one of the orphanage children. There were
         ten of us went out to Peter's school every day. And
         because I was talented with gimlets and hairpins, he
         took an interest in me. Bought me raincoats and fur-
         lined boots and leather helmets with flaps that came
         down over my ears and buttoned under my chin and
         kept me snug and dry. And when the Christian
         Brothers released me into the world, he got me a job
         with an electrical contractor and sent me to a technical
         college at night and encouraged me in every possible
         way to get my diploma. And when I got it, he arranged
         a job for me in his school. And for these endless and
         tireless kindnesses I have always been grateful, most
         grateful, to Peter. And here I now am. And there the
         story ends. And that's the truth, so help me God. If one

admits that there is no absolute truth, would the panel agree that the melodramatic Victorian novelists reveal a concept of reality that does indeed have a kind of bizarre authenticity? Doctor Heimerstammer?

Pause.

SARAH Are youse definitely leaving tomorrow?

SHANE At full tide, lass, with a fresh wind and God willing.

SARAH Do you like living in Dublin?

SHANE No.

SARAH Why don't you leave it then?

SHANE I may. Soon.

SARAH There's nothing to stop you, is there?

SHANE I'm not sure.

SARAH A girl, maybe?

SHANE If it's anything, it's a spook. A spook called Obligation, sired by Duty out of Liability. Daughter, may he niver cross your gintle path. Do you believe in ghosts?

She smiles.

SARAH Philly does laugh at me.

SHANE Why?

SARAH He says I be only imagining things.

SHANE Have you seen 'things'?

SARAH Maybe I have.

SHANE What have you seen?

SARAH You'll laugh, too.

SHANE Never when I'm working.

SARAH Well . . .

SHANE Go on!

SARAH Once I went into the byre. It was evening. It was just getting dark.

SHANE And?

SARAH And there the cow was, chained to the post; and I had the bucket and the milking-stool in my hand; and when I went round to the far side of the cow, sitting there milking into a pandy was this wee fat, bald man, with a checked shirt and an ugly, sweaty face.

37

SHANE Peter!

*She bursts out laughing at the accuracy of the descrip-
tion.*

SARAH God forgive you!
SHANE Who else!
SARAH Now I don't know where I was at.
SHANE He was milking into a pan.
SARAH A pandy, you clown you! Not a pan. And anyway I
went screaming into the house and dragged Philly out
and pushed him into the byre before me. And there
was nobody there but the cow. But —
SHANE But the air was still heavy with the bald man's after-
shave lotion!
SARAH But the cow had been milked. There wasn't a drop in her.
SHANE Never!
SARAH Honest to God.
SHANE What did Philly say?
SARAH He blamed the calf.
SHANE What calf?
SARAH There was a young calf in the byre, too.
SHANE In a checked shirt?

She laughs. They both laugh.

SARAH I knew you wouldn't believe me.

Pause. He goes on working.

This place will be wild dead again when you leave.
SHANE A little less hectic maybe.
SARAH I'll miss you.
SHANE People always warm to me after I've told them I'm a
bastard.
SARAH When you're not about the house here, when you're
down below at the tent, I do watch you all the time
through the French binoculars.

Pause.

Peter goes for a walk at ten o'clock every night along the white strand. When he goes out tonight I'll go down to the tent to you.

SHANE Sorry. Rotary meeting tonight, luv.

SARAH I want to lie with you, engineer.

He stops working.

SHANE I snore in my sleep. And my elbows are like daggers.

SARAH Will you lie with me?

SHANE Philly.

SARAH He's no good to me.

SHANE He's your husband.

SARAH Will you lie with me?

SHANE No, Sarah.

SARAH Why not? Tell me why not?

PETER *enters left.*

PETER You still at that thing? Hello, Sarah. Is the dinner ready? I'm just ravenous. (*As she runs off right*) The men are on their way down. (*To* SHANE) Not got it fixed yet?

SHANE Not yet.

PETER Can it be done?

SHANE I think so.

PETER What's wrong with it anyhow?

SHANE Age.

PETER Looks like a collector's item to me.

PETER *sits on the ground and relaxes.*

If you think teaching's tiring, spend a morning cutting turf. My shoulders and the backs of my legs are just aching. No job for an old codger like me. Ahhhhh. That's good.

SHANE Where's the bog?

PETER Beyond the ruins of the old monastery. I showed it to you yesterday — just beyond where we had the picnic. My God, it's beautiful up there, Shane: the sun and the fresh wind from the sea and the sky alive with larks and the smell of heather.

SHANE Heaven.

PETER What's that?

SHANE Heavenly.

PETER It is. Really.

SHANE Divine.

PETER Are you being flippant?

SHANE Deadly earnest.

PETER Interesting the difference between Joe and Philly up there. Joe's all lather and earnestness; grunting and heaving and so obviously labouring. And Philly — he doesn't make a sound; but you should see him cutting that turf out of the bank — swift, clean, not a superfluous gesture. Sheer delight to watch him. Poor old Manus and myself messing along behind him. Lord, how I'd love a swim before we eat but I'm too damn lazy to walk down and up again. Did you have a bathe?

SHANE Not yet.

PETER We'll go after lunch. Fantastic weather. Never had a holiday like this in my life. Ever. And never saw a holiday fly as quickly. (*He sits up*) Manus was talking to me up there. Wants us to come back at Christmas. Spend the Christmas holidays here with him. He was very pressing. (*Pause*) I think it's a nice idea — Christmas on an island.

> SHANE *suddenly stops working at the gramophone. He slips his left arm out of his sleeve and tucks it into his belt.*

SHANE Be Jaysus, Shane boy, you're a quare comedian. You should be on the stage. Like me. Look at the act I have — the simple, upright, hardworking island peasant holding on manfully to the *real* values in life, sustained by a thousand-year-old culture, preserving for my people a really worthwhile inheritance.

> PETER *looks around nervously.*

PETER Shhh!

SHANE (*Recklessly*) D'you see that bed you're lying on, sir? Three hundred and forty-seven sailors went down with the ship that bed came off. And that ring on your finger was on the finger of a young airman when his plane plunged down on the very spot you're standing on. We're poor people, sir. We survive only because of other people's disasters — musha, God help them.

PETER That's very mean, very rotten!

SHANE And now, as a di-varsion, I'll tell youse the old tale of the white-headed harper ·from the townland of Ballymaglin in the barony of Kildare.

PETER He couldn't have been kinder to us.

SHANE True. So we're grateful, most grateful.

PETER And he genuinely wants us back.

SHANE Of course he does. Because we give support to his illusion that the place isn't a cemetery. But it is. And he knows it. The place and his way of life and everything he believes in and all he touches — dead, finished, spent. And when he finally faces that, he's liable to become dangerous. You sympathise with him because you're a romantic, too. Where was I this summer? As a matter of fact I spent four days in a war museum. Fascinating place.

PETER I thought you enjoyed it.

SHANE You never listen to me.

PETER You do like it here. I know you do.

SHANE You see?

PETER And they like you. They all like you.

SHANE Which of me?

PETER All I know is that they've been consistently kind, that they've made these few days memorable, and that they've asked us back. And I want to come back.

SHANE Then come.

PETER With you.

SHANE I've stopped making plans.

PETER I'm not asking much — a week at Christmas, that's all.

SHANE You have the gauche subtlety of an insurance man: only tuppence a week — for a million years.

PETER Is a week so precious to you?

SHANE Christmas is six months away. Does our lease extend to that?

PETER Shane, I'm not like you —

SHANE Peter the Sincere.

PETER — I can't live casually any more; I'm too old for that. I've got to the stage when I need a — a — a modest permanence.

SHANE Six months ahead is greedy.

PETER Not at my time of day. And I'm not looking for a commitment. I've never asked you for a commitment, have I? Just a reasonable expectation.

SHANE The ledgers say we've had ten years. That's quite a stretch. When are obligations fully satisfied?

PETER Don't make me grovel, Shane.

SHANE I couldn't stop you.

PETER Please say you'll come. I'm asking you.

SHANE *(Steps back from gramophone)* Ah! That's it! Fixed!

PETER You owe it to me, Shane.

SHANE I owe it to *you*?

PETER You do. You know you do.

SHANE *goes towards the kitchen.*

I don't mean money — material things — but in loyalty, devotion, dedication, concern, kindness —

SHANE Love?

PETER Goddamnit, yes! Love, Shane, love, love — all I have is invested in you — everything — for the best years of my life. There must be some return. It's not extravagant to expect something.

SHANE It is.

PETER Not from someone who isn't as callous as you! But then your affections have always been as uncertain as your origins!

SHANE *dashes into the kitchen, searches feverishly in presses for a record.* PETER, *genuinely shocked at himself, follows him.*

Shane, I'm sorry — my God I'm sorry — I'm sorry, Shane — I didn't mean a word of it — I'm tired — I'm jittery — I'm jealous of Sarah, of Philly, of everyone — forgive me,

Shane, please forgive me.

SHANE has found a record. He speaks at an almost hysterical speed and pitch.

SHANE If you were going to end your days on a barren island, Sir
Peter, what record would you choose?

He runs out to the street. PETER follows him.

What record would I choose? Well I think my first choice
would be an ancient Gaelic folk-song that I first heard
sung by an old man on an island off the west coast of
County Donegal, a song called — (*Reading record*) — *Oh!
Susanna*, arranged and played by Harry Dudley and his
band. And why would you choose that record, Sir Peter?
PETER I'm genuinely sorry.
SHANE Because it reminds me of a memorable holiday I once
had on a heavenly island one divine summer.

*He has wound up the gramophone. He puts the record on.
The band plays an introductory line. Enter PHILLY and
JOE left.*

Marvellous! Let's have *Oh! Susanna* to bring back
happy memories of that divine summer.
PHILLY You have it going, engineer?
JOE Good man, Seán.

*PHILLY is wearing a straw hat. As SHANE begins to sing
and dance to the music he picks up a stick from the ground
and snatches the straw hat and puts it on the back of his
head. Now he does a song-and-dance routine.*

SHANE (*Sings*) 'I come from Alabama
With my banjo on my knee.
I'm going to Louisiana
My true love for to see!'

PHILLY claps in time with the music. JOE joins him.

JOE   Good on you, boy!

PHILLY Get up there, Peter!

SHANE   'It rained all night
        The day I left,
        The weather it was dry — '

        He dances across to PETER, *holds out his hands in invitation.*

        Sir Peter?

JOE   Ya-hooooooooooo!

SHANE   ' — the sun so hot
        I froze to death,
        Susanna, don't you cry.'

        Hands out to JOE.

        Come on, Joe.

JOE   You're doing great by yourself.

SHANE   'Oh! Susanna,
        Don't you cry for me,
        I come from Alabama
        With my banjo on my knee.'

        As the band plays a link passage between verses SHANE *catches* PHILLY's *hand.*

        Come on, Philly. Dance with me.

JOE   Go on, Philly boy! Give us a buck-lep!

        PHILLY *releases his hand roughly.*

PHILLY Go to hell!

        SARAH *enters right as the second verse begins.* SHANE *sings and dances.*

SHANE   'I had a dream
        The other night
        When everything was still,

I thought I saw Susanna
A-coming down the hill.
The buckwheat cake was in her mouth,
A tear was in her eye,
Says I'm coming from the south,
Susanna, don't you cry.
Oh! Susanna,
Don't you cry for me . . . '

When she enters SHANE *dances across to her, catches her and swings her round. She slaps his face viciously — howls of laughter from* JOE *and* PHILLY.

JOE Jaysus, that's a quare uppercut, Seán!
PHILLY Give him another! Another! Another!
JOE Beat the head off him, girl!
PETER Stop it! Stop it!

SHANE *pretends the slap has sent him reeling. He recovers. He goes after* SARAH *again as she goes into the kitchen and then into her bedroom. As he pretends to follow her into the kitchen* PHILLY *trips him at the door. He falls. The laughter rises. He gets up — without breaking his song — and pretends to stagger after her.* PHILLY *shoves him roughly back. He falls against* JOE. JOE *pushes him away. He falls against* PETER. PETER *shies away from him and looks around in rising panic. He lurches towards* PHILLY. PHILLY *punches him. He falls heavily. He makes no effort to rise. He just lies there, singing.* PHILLY *punches him again and again.*

PHILLY Dance, you bastard! Dance! Dance!
JOE Yip-eeeeeeeeee!

PETER *can endure no more. He goes to the gramophone, stops it, takes off the record. Silence.*

What did you do that for, Peter?

SHANE *rises, finds his hat and cane, strikes an exit attitude.*

SHANE Ta-ra-rah.

PETER smashes the record.

JOE What in the name of God did you want to go and break the good record for, man?
PETER I thought he — I was afraid he'd hurt himself.
JOE Seán? Jaysus, it'd take more than that to hurt aul' Seán. Yes, boy?

He ruffles his hair as he passes him.

Should be on the stage, man. A buck like you would make a fortune going round the halls. (*Now in the kitchen*) Any sign of the dinner, Sarah? Sarah!

SHANE *is looking at his hand.* PHILLY *stands watching.*

PETER Are you hurt?
SHANE I'm fine.
PETER Show me.
SHANE I'm alright.
PETER Let me see.
SHANE I'm telling you — I'm fine, fine.
PHILLY We were only beginning to warm up there, weren't we? (*To* PETER) You should see us when we get going full steam.

He goes towards the kitchen, stops at the door.

What are you doing this evening?
PETER We're going —
PHILLY Shane.
SHANE What?
PHILLY I'll be shooting lobster-pots on the east side later on. Come out for the run. I'll show you the caves the aul' fella was telling you about.
PETER We're going for a swim this afternoon.
PHILLY (*To* SHANE) About five o'clock. As soon as we finish in the bog. (*Laughs*) We're making a farmer out of your

nanny — aren't we, Peter?

He laughs again and goes into the kitchen.

PETER Let me see.
SHANE It's nothing.
PETER It looks deep. Is it sore?
SHANE A bit.
PETER Put this (*handkerchief*) round it in the meantime.
SHANE Stop fussing.
PETER Come down to the tent. I've got iodine in my rucksack. Where's your jacket?
SHANE Did I have it?
PETER You had it this morning.
SHANE Yes — it's behind the kitchen door.

Pause.

PETER We'll get it later. Come on. That could turn nasty.

They go off left. JOE, *who has been setting the table, sees them go.*

JOE Where's the two off to?
PHILLY To the tent.
JOE Sure the dinner's ready. (*Calls*) Peter! Seán! The dinner's ready!
PHILLY They'll be back.
JOE A handy man all the same, the engineer. I thought the machine was finished. Did he fix the outboard?
PHILLY Aye.
JOE What was wrong with it?
PHILLY Something about the belt. I didn't understand it.
JOE A handy fella to have about a place. Must have a right head on him.
PHILLY What did you make of Peter at the turf?
JOE You're a bugger, too.
PHILLY Me?
JOE Don't think I didn't see you — plunging the spade down within half an inch of his hand every time.

47

PHILLY Quarter of an inch.

JOE Mercy to God you didn't take the hand off him.

PHILLY But I didn't.

JOE And him killing himself trying to keep up with you.

PHILLY I knew what I was at.

JOE Just as well.

PHILLY I think he knew, too.

MANUS *enters quickly from the left.*

MANUS That mongrel they tried to drown — he's outside at the henhouse. Give me my stick.

JOE Did he kill any?

MANUS He's still outside — trying to scratch his way under the door.

PHILLY *lifts a hay fork.*

PHILLY I'll settle him.

MANUS Give it to me. I'll get him. I'll wait 'till he's cornered inside.

He goes off with the fork.

JOE Mind he doesn't turn on you, Father! (*To* PHILLY) I seen him at the gable last night. Sarah throws him an odd crust of bread; that's what brings him about.

PHILLY She feeds him?

JOE She leaves an odd scrap for him.

PHILLY He damn near killed a lamb the day before yesterday!

JOE A dog's something we could do with ourselves. I was thinking, Philly, maybe if Sarah fed him regular —

PHILLY He was never a working dog.

JOE He was a nice dog.

PHILLY Good for nothing. Unless it's a pet you want! (*Yelping, off*) That's him anyway.

SARAH *enters from bedroom.*

SARAH What's that? What's the noise?

PHILLY We're waiting for the dinner. When you're ready.

SARAH Is it the dog that's yelping?

PHILLY Did you think it was the bucks below in the tent? Your friends?

SARAH No friends of mine.

PHILLY A fine long morning alone with the engineer, hadn't you?

SARAH It didn't bring you running back to the house.

MANUS *enters.*

JOE Did you get him?

MANUS I got one lunge at him.

PHILLY Did you kill him?

SARAH Kill who? My father's dog?

MANUS He made a jump for the window. I got him in the neck.

PHILLY He got away?

MANUS Dragging himself by the front paws.

PHILLY You botch everything!

MANUS He made over the wall and up the hill. I didn't get a second go. He'll not last long, though.

SARAH There's no harm in that dog.

MANUS He was at the hens. Where's the strangers?

JOE (*To* SARAH) The engineer fixed the outboard, too.

PHILLY And her radio.

MANUS I don't understand a word that young lad says. Peter has more sense to him. He was asking me up there could they come back at Christmas.

JOE Here in a tent in December? Bloody mad!

MANUS That's what I said to him. What I think he was angling for was for me to ask them to stay here in the house.

JOE That's more sensible.

SARAH There's no room for them in this house or in any other house here either.

JOE Jaysus, you're in a bad twist.

PHILLY (*To* MANUS) What did you say? What did you say?

MANUS Well, I told him that —

Sound of dog baying. Silence in the kitchen. SHANE *runs on to the street. The dog bays again.* SHANE *lifts his head and bays back.*

JOE That's no dog!
SARAH It's him.
MANUS Who?

JOE goes to the door.

JOE It's Seán! Christ, would you look at him! Yes, Seán! Watch out or you'll get the fork in you, too.

SHANE comes into the kitchen.

SHANE Single yelp shatters fragile peace. Acute unease on paradise island. War thought imminent. All men over seventeen report for military service. Gentlemen — and good lady — my friend is detained but will join us presently. He asks you not to wait for him. Is luncheon served? Bless us, O Lord, for these and all Thy other gifts which from Thy bounty we are about to receive.
PHILLY (*Laughing*) Amen to that, engineer! Amen to that!

Blackout.

ACT TWO

Scene One

Later that same evening. SARAH, JOE, MANUS *and* PETER *are playing Solo.* MANUS *has his cards on a breadboard on his knee.* JOE *is playing a hand.*

JOE   Come on, Father. Your lead. Play, man, play. Go down like a soldier.

MANUS   How many have you got?

PETER   He needs one more.

JOE   I'm home and dry. Youse might as well pack it in — youse are beat.

    MANUS leads.

MANUS   That's the best I can do.

JOE   And it's not much good. Yes, Sarah?

    SARAH *plays a card.* JOE *looks into her hand.*

The Jack's better than that.

SARAH   Is it?

JOE   Is it! What d'you think's trump? Take that up and play the Jack.

    She obeys.

Peter?

PETER   I'm afraid he's through.

    He plays a card.

JOE Covered by a darling wee ace of trump! And that gives me nine! And game! And you're welcome to the rest of them. Pay up! Pay up!

MANUS The cards are that old he knows every scratch on the back of them.

SARAH *rises from the table.*

SARAH That's me out.

PETER (*To* JOE) You owed me a penny from the last hand. That's us quits.

JOE *pushes a handful of coins across the table to* SARAH.

JOE Here, Sarah. That'll stake you for a couple of hands more.

SARAH I'm not playing.

JOE You can't break up the game.

SARAH Finished.

JOE Come on. Be a sport.

SARAH Are you deaf as well as thick!

JOE Jaysus, you're in quare humour. (*To others*) What's biting her all day? Like a bag of bloody weasels.

MANUS *rises.*

MANUS It's getting dark anyway.

JOE Three more hands — that's all. Two more.

MANUS We've had enough for one night.

JOE A couple of hands of poker to finish up. Right, Peter?

PETER I'm agreeable.

JOE Be a sport, Father. Sit down.

MANUS No, no more tonight. You get stiff sitting too long.

JOE Damn poor losers, the lot of you.

PETER *rises.*

PETER It's hard to be a good loser when the cards are marked.

JOE Sticks and stones will break my bones. But the truth is it's the skill that counts in the end. And you haven't got it, boys.

SARAH *lights the lamp.*

MANUS Is the milking not going to be done?

JOE Is the bucket scalded?

SARAH There.

JOE It's hardly worthwhile milking these nights.

PETER You can't lift lobster-pots in the dark, can you?

MANUS Not unless you have to.

PETER What I'm thinking is — Philly and Shane should be back, shouldn't they?

MANUS There'll be no hurry on Philly. He doesn't know what time means when he's out in a boat.

PETER He's going fishing again tonight, isn't he? I mean he'll come home first and then go out again?

JOE He'll probably leave Seán off at the far slip and head out again by himself. He'll hardly come up here. (*To* SARAH) Did he take a piece with him?

SARAH He did.

JOE You'll not see him 'till morning then. (*As he leaves with the bucket*) What about another wee hand later?

PETER The next game we'll have will be at Christmas — and then we'll play with *my* marked cards.

JOE *laughs and leaves.*

MANUS (*To* SARAH) Are you making supper?

No answer.

Sarah!

SARAH What?

MANUS Are you making no supper?

SARAH If you want it.

MANUS Surely we want it. Isn't it supper time? (*To* PETER) When are you leaving tomorrow?

PETER Before lunch. We'll need to be on the road early to get lifts.

MANUS Joe'll take you out. He's hoping there'll be a letter for him at the post-office.

53

PETER *stands at the door looking out over the sea.*

PETER I imagine, if you could see them, they're trying to escape now.

MANUS Who?

PETER The monks and the girl.

MANUS Them. Hah! They're wasting their time. They'll make nothing of it.

PETER I can't tell you how I hate going, Manus.

MANUS You were lucky in the weather.

PETER Absolutely lovely. (*View*)

MANUS The man in the radio says it's the warmest June since the turn of the century.

PETER It's not the weather; it's the . . . the calm, the stability, the self-possession. Everything has its own good pace. No panics, no feverish gropings. A dependable routine — that's what you have.

MANUS The weather makes all the difference.

PETER I envy you, Manus: the sea, the land, fishing, turf-cutting, milking, a house built by your great-grand-father, two strong sons to succeed you — everything's so damned constant. You're part of a permanence. You're a fortunate man.

MANUS You wouldn't live here all the same.

PETER I could.

MANUS Why would you want to be wrestling with the elements here and you with your clean indoor job and your good salary? And in another while you'll be sitting back and drawing your pension. Is it sixty or sixty-five you retire at?

PETER No pension for me, Manus.

MANUS Why's that?

PETER I gave up the clean, indoor, pensionable job years ago.

SARAH The engineer's a liar then!

PETER Shane?

SARAH He said you taught in the same school as him.

PETER I did. For a while. Then the principal and I had a row —

SARAH About the engineer?

PETER — and I haven't taught in a school since.

SARAH Why couldn't you get into another school? Why?

PETER Oh I work. Every Wednesday I play the piano in the lounge of the Imperial Hotel during afternoon teas. And I take pupils — I have a few pupils. And when times are really thin, d'you know what I do, Manus? You'd never guess. I tune pianos. Yes. I have a very efficient bicycle that takes me round the whole of Dublin. And in the spring and summer I venture as far afield as Wicklow. Tuning pianos . . .

MANUS As long as you make a living.

PETER Between us we manage. We have enough.

MANUS *goes to the dresser. Embarrassment makes him formal.*

MANUS Peter, it has been a good thing for us to have you here with us. You came at a time when we were hungry for new voices.

PETER If anyone's grateful —

MANUS *holds up his hand.*

MANUS Your educated company was my pleasure, and Shane himself was more entertainment for the young people than the instruments he set going again. As a token of my pleasure and gratitude I want you to accept this clock. There's a bit of a dent on the top but she's a damn fine time-keeper.

PETER I couldn't, Manus. I really couldn't —

MANUS Take it. Don't offend me. No more to be said.

PETER It's — gosh, it's — it's too much. It really is. We ate here, we took your milk and vegetables and —

MANUS No more. No more. She came off a Dutch freighter in '43. And if I hadn't got it, some other man would.

PETER I'm most grateful. Thank you very much.

MANUS You're welcome. That's it now — we'll talk no more about it. I'll tell you something now, Peter, that I've always had in my heart: man, it's a thing I'd love to be able to do — play the piano. You haven't any pupils with one hand, have you?

PETER One would be enough for most of them. What

happened to it?

MANUS Butte, Montana; in the copper mines there. We were working on our backs in a three-foot tunnel and the mine-face came down on us. And that was it. (*To* SARAH) I'll take more tea.

PETER Was it painful?

MANUS It was sorer getting used to being without it. Lucky I was a healthy buck or I mightn't be here today.

PETER Were you alone at the time?

MANUS There were six of us. Working a fourteen-hour shift. We earned our money hard. And damn little sense we had for holding on to it. I went away with fifteen dollars in my pocket, sir, and I came back with fifteen dollars. You could say I held my own.

PETER You manage wonderfully.

SARAH Tell him the truth.

MANUS More tea, I said.

SARAH When he came back from America he had his two arms.

MANUS That'll do you.

SARAH Two arms and a glib tongue and a roving eye he had.

MANUS Shut up.

SARAH And at the back of the hill there was a gentle young girl called Rosie Dubh — Rosie Duffy — living with two aul' uncles that never spoke and never washed and never lit a fire.

MANUS Shut your mouth, woman!

SARAH They were backward people. They never went to the shop, never mixed with the neighbours, and young Rosie was never out of the island in her life. And when the buck came home from the States he went smelling about the back of the hill. Oh they all say he was a smart buck, able with the tongue. And he got Rosie Dubh pregnant.

MANUS I'll break your neck!

SARAH And as soon as she told him, off he skited to England. And that's where Philly was born, back there, delivered by two filthy aul' men that kicked her about as soon as she was fit to be on her feet. And after twelve months he came home — God knows why — maybe he was running away from some English girl. And the night he arrived down at the harbour there, the two uncles were waiting for him with knives they use here for gutting herring. And that's how the arm was lost — in that fight. And he married Rosie then because he had to — he was stuck here; there's no living in England for one-armed labourers. But by that time Rosie was past caring. And a month after her second son was born she went out for a walk along the cliffs on the east side and was never seen since.

MANUS You're a foul-mouthed —

SARAH Joe doesn't know the truth. But Philly does. And he'll never forgive you for it. And if he can't father a family, you're the cause of it.

MANUS Bitch!

SARAH *runs out and off right. Pause.*

There's ways and ways of telling every story. Every story has seven faces. And there's things shouldn't be said before a stranger.

In case the word offends PETER *he touches him on the shoulder.*

When I came home from Montana, after all the whores that lived in the camp, she was that — that — that — she called me Mister Manus! Jesus, me that was born and reared not three miles from her own doorstep!

PETER It's none of my business, Manus.

MANUS I came home to marry her. That's what brought me back. And before I left London I had a place ready to bring her and the boy back to. It wasn't much of a place but it was better than the uncles' hovel.

PETER No need to talk about it.

MANUS When they jumped me below at the harbour I had the wedding ring in my pocket. That's what brought me back — I'd gathered a couple of pounds to start us off. It might have been better to leave her be. She'd got used to being alone in the twelve months. And she had the baby. And this (*arm*), somehow it made her uneasy with me.

PETER The body was never found?

MANUS Many's the thing the sea gave me but it held on to her. But she's lying about Philly. He knows the story but he knows the whole story. He holds nothing against me. Not Philly.

PETER She's been upset all day.

MANUS Damned right he doesn't. He knows the whole story.

JOE enters left.

JOE Christ, Father, you'd get more milk from a billy-goat than that aul' heifer. Look at that. It's this drought. If we don't get rain soon we'll be drinking black tea. Sarah! The strainer!

PETER Is this it?

JOE The boys is back: I could hear Seán singing over at the far slip. Jaysus, he's a jolly sailor. I wonder how the pots were. D'you know what lobsters are making now? Twenty shillings a pound! That's what you Dublin fellas are paying! Twenty shillings! And if poor aul' Philly gets half that from the dealer out, he thinks he's doing great.

PETER I think I'll go for my walk and then get some things packed up. See you both in the morning.

JOE What about your milk?

PETER Shane'll take it. All we need is a cupful for breakfast.

JOE There'll be a canful. We're not that hard pressed.

PETER See you tomorrow, Manus.

MANUS Goodnight. Goodnight.

PETER goes off left. JOE picks up teapot.

JOE Is it cold?

MANUS It shouldn't be.

JOE Was the clock stopped?

MANUS What?

JOE The clock — were you working at it?

MANUS I gave it to Peter. He must have forgotten it.

JOE I'll bring it down when I drink this.

MANUS Shane can take it.

> JOE *pours tea and sits.*

JOE It's not going to be as lively after tomorrow. (*Pause*) You'll miss the antics of the engineer about the place. Jaysus, he's as good as a concert, that fella. (*Pause*) Aye, it'll not be as lively after they go.

MANUS Did you write to Anna yet?

JOE To Anna? To Anna Con? Where would I get the time? Sunday, maybe, when Sarah's doing nothing.

MANUS Have you got her address?

> JOE *takes a scrap of paper from his pocket.*

JOE She wrote it out for me. It's 17 . . . 17 . . . (*He hands it to* MANUS) Christ, she's an awkward fist.

MANUS Get me the pen and paper.

JOE You? Damnit I'm at my supper, man.

MANUS Hurry up. You can post it tomorrow when you go out.

JOE Jaysus, Father, there's no news, unless the heifer going dry —

MANUS Now.

> JOE *gets the pen and paper.* MANUS *settles himself at the kitchen table.*

JOE You need to be in a humour for writing letters. I'm in no humour, I can tell you.

MANUS What date's this?

JOE Saturday.

MANUS Date.

JOE I don't know the date. Jaysus, the date! How would I know the date! Jaysus.

MANUS Doesn't matter. Go ahead. (*Pause*) Well?

JOE Well what?

MANUS Tell me what you want me to say.

JOE How would I know! It's you that's writing it.

MANUS 'Dear Anna, my father is writing this letter for me.'

59

JOE   That's smart. She'll know it's not me, won't she?

MANUS 'The weather has not broken since you left and for the past three days we have been carrying water from Big Anthony's well.' What else?

JOE   The turf's all cut.

MANUS 'The turf's all cut.'

JOE   And Philly's hammering away at the salmon and lobster. Two strangers from Dublin were here. They had a tent below at the green. They are leaving tomorrow. Every day since you left I go into your house and look about it. Sometimes I sit down for a while. Yesterday I was sitting at your fireplace and I thought I heard you . . . . What in the name of God is there to write about in this place!

MANUS 'Anna, I want you to come back and marry me.'

JOE   What are you at?

MANUS 'I will call on the priest tomorrow.'

JOE   Jaysus.

MANUS 'We will make out alright. Bring Con back with you.'

JOE   Jaysus, Father.

MANUS 'I am enclosing the fare for the two of you.'

JOE   Fare? I haven't twenty pounds! I haven't twenty pence!

MANUS 'I mean this, Anna. Please come home and marry me. As soon as possible. Please.' How do I sign it?

JOE   What do you mean?

MANUS How do I finish off?

JOE   Manus.

MANUS It's from you!

JOE   Joe, then.

MANUS Is that all?

JOE   In haste, Joe. Kindly excuse writing and spelling. They are not mine.

MANUS *takes money from his pocket, puts it into the envelope, addresses envelope.*

MANUS That'll take them home.

JOE   Christ, Father, she'll fall down with the shock. Christ, what'll she say? Rub out that bit about the hot weather — Christ, she'll think I've sun-stroke. Holy Christ,

Father, d'you think she'd ever have me? Oh my God, Sarah could never have written as powerful a letter as that.

MANUS *puts the letter on the mantelpiece.*

MANUS Tell the priest tomorrow that you want it fixed up next month at the latest.

JOE Father, if she takes me, Father, there'll be no happier man in Ireland.

SARAH *enters from the right.*

Sarah, I've written to Anna. I've asked her to marry me.

SARAH *addresses* MANUS *only. She speaks very softly.*

SARAH Would you like to have a look at your son? Would you like to see the bull that's going to sire your grand-children and bring back life to this graveyard?

MANUS What's this?

SARAH No, you don't want to see. Philly's the prince. Philly's the hero. Philly's the apple of your blind eye. And it's easier to blame me, isn't it? I'm the barren one. My womb bears no crop. Like the lower field good seed's wasted on me. The worst mistake your Philly could have made, wasn't it, to marry a sterile woman?

MANUS What are you trying to say?

SARAH That he's down there in the boathouse at the far slip, your Philly, my husband. That he's down there with that Dublin tramp, Shane. That they're stripped naked. That he's doing for the tramp what he couldn't do for me. That's what I'm trying to say. And that if you're the great king of Inishkeen, you'll kill them both — that's what I'm saying.

Quick blackout.

ACT TWO

Scene Two

A short time later. JOE *is sitting at the kitchen table, his head in his hands.* MANUS *is in the airplane seat, facing upstage, as he was in the opening scene.* SARAH *is looking out the window.*
   The lamp is turned down low. The kitchen is almost dark. The street outside is bright with moonlight.

SARAH   He's coming. He's alone. He has his jacket across his shoulder and his shoes in his left hand. He's stopped now. He's looking about him at everything clear in the moonlight. He's saying to himself, 'My God, it's heavenly'.

JOE   What are you going to do, Father?

SARAH   He's stooping down. He's picking up something. A stone. He's skimming it across the top of the water. He's moving again. He's coming.

JOE   Tell me what you're going to do.

SARAH   What are you going to do, Manus?

JOE   No one's going to lay a finger on him.

SARAH   What about the herring knives, Manus?

       JOE *jumps up.*

JOE   No one's using no knives here. Two's to blame or no one's to blame.

SARAH   This is none of your business, boy.

JOE   I'm warning you, woman. Put none of your poison into my father's head.

SARAH   Manus knows his own mind. He knows what he'll do. Shhh! Quiet! I think — aye, he's singing! Listen and you'll hear him singing. He's a happy buck, the engineer. Do you hear him singing, Manus?

MANUS People have lived here for hundreds of years, thousands of years.

SARAH He's in the hollow. I've lost him now.

MANUS There were people here before Christ was born.

JOE (*To* SARAH) You could have made a mistake.

SARAH I could have made a mistake, Manus.

JOE Maybe their clothes were wet. Philly wouldn't walk the length of himself in wet socks.

SARAH Maybe they were wet, Manus.

JOE And it's black dark in the boathouse. How could you see in the dark?

SARAH He's talking sense, Manus. How could I be sure in the dark? What do you think, Manus? Is there doubt in your mind?

> *In the distance right we can hear* SHANE *singing 'Oh! Susanna' very faintly, getting louder slowly.*

MANUS The gun.

SARAH He's on the path. He's coming. He's coming. Listen. He's coming.

MANUS Give me the gun.

> SARAH *gets the gun and gives it to him. He leaves it beside him on the ground.*

JOE Jaysus, he can't use that!

SARAH He's here, Manus.

JOE (*To* MANUS) They're going in the morning. They'll be gone this time tomorrow and —

SARAH Stay out of it!

JOE And you'll never see them again.

SARAH (*To* MANUS) Mind — if you haven't the stomach, I have!

JOE You can't use the gun, Father. For God's sake. You —

MANUS Shut up!

JOE I'll — I'll — I'll get Peter. Peter'll stop you.

> JOE *dashes out and off left.*

SARAH 'Peter'll stop you.' For a while there he didn't know how he was going to escape, did he? But he's only a boy. This time you'll be a man, Manus. This time.

SHANE enters right. SARAH goes to the fireplace and pretends to be busy. SHANE goes into the kitchen.

SHANE *Oíche mhaith díobh agus bail ó Dhia ar an obair agus go n-éirigh an bóthair libh.* How's that then? Philly taught me. Isn't that pretty good? Yes?

SARAH Very good.

SHANE I'm not finished yet. *Bíonn adharca fada ar buaibh thar lár!* There are long horns on cows far away. Which means far away hills look green. Purest Donegal Irish, untouched by human hand. (*Softly, to* SARAH) Is he asleep?

SARAH Are you asleep, Manus?

MANUS No.

SARAH He's wide awake. What did you think of the caves?

SHANE Never saw them. By the time we got the pots lifted the skipper decided the tide was too far in. He said a fool can row into a cave in low water but it takes a wise man to get out when the tide's full. I'm sure there's an Irish equivalent for that. Something like: The widow-woman with three old hens makes potato bread more quickly than the grey seal grows feathers.

SARAH So what did you do?

SHANE After we lifted the pots? Your worthy husband brought me on a wonderful carefree cruise and pointed out the precise location of all the wartime disasters. We cunningly sidestepped the Monks below and headed for the Stags where the Dutch freighter went down and the point where the British tanker broke up and the beach where the sailors were washed in. It was a jolly, jolly trip, complete with gruesome details. When curt Captain Philly starts talking, there's no stopping him. There must be an idiom for that, too: When the silent snipe flies high on a midsummer's night, the beggarman with the red whiskers cries into the water at the broken ford. No. Obviously spurious.

Too ornate. Too wordy — (*After a quick look round*) — just like me.

SARAH Did you go for a swim?

SHANE Yes.

SARAH Where?

SHANE At the far slip.

SARAH Before you went out?

SHANE When we came back.

SARAH In the dark?

SHANE In the moonlight.

SARAH Just a while ago?

He looks at her for a second, then turns to MANUS.

SHANE You're quiet, Manus. What did they do to you up in the bog?

SARAH Half an hour ago?

MANUS There was a niggerman came to this island once when I was a boy. He arrived on a December morning, this niggerman, and he was carrying a caseful of holy pictures that he was selling round the country.

SHANE That's what Peter and I may end up doing.

MANUS And the day he came in, a storm broke and he was stranded here. And there lived at that time in a bothy of a place down behind the harbour an old couple by the name of Boyle, Andy Boyle and Susan Boyle, and they were both reduced to half their size with the pains of rheumatism.

SHANE And he laid hands on their bent heads and —

SARAH Listen!

SHANE Sorry.

MANUS And that's where the niggerman shacked up, in the bothy with the Boyles. And one morning my father was gathering kelp on the beach and he heard the shouts and the roars coming from the bothy, and out hobbled old Andy, and behind him Susan, and they roared to my father, 'Seize the niggerman! He's a thief. He's robbed us of all our money! He stole our five golden sovereigns!' And with that, out of the bothy leaped the niggerman and off with him over the hill.

SHANE All niggers is thieves, man.

SARAH Quicker, Manus.

MANUS Well, sir, the men of the place soon caught him, and they bound his hands and his feet, and they wrapped a net about him, and they carried him above to the schoolhouse, and true enough they found the five golden sovereigns in his pocket. And then they had to settle on his punishment. And the punishment they settled on was this.

SHANE I'm breathless.

MANUS Bound as he was, they harnessed him by a long rope to an old donkey. Then they pumped linseed oil down into the donkey's ears. And for a full day, sir, until it dropped dead, the mad donkey dragged that nigger-man across the length and breadth of this island. Then they rowed that niggerman out to the mainland and dumped him there. And them that dumped him said all he was fit to do was inch away from them on all fours, sideways like a crab.

SARAH That's what happened. What do you make of that story, engineer?

MANUS All he took was five sovereigns.

SHANE An obscene story.

SARAH And he was only a travelling man.

SHANE So what's the moral? Don't attempt to peddle religion to savages?

SARAH (*To* MANUS) Savages! Listen!

MANUS I'm looking for no moral, sir. But I'm thinking the men above in the schoolhouse estimated that it was a fair punishment for a thief.

SHANE And no doubt they had their reasons. Did Peter collect the milk?

MANUS And I'm thinking you did a worse thing than the niggerman.

SHANE Me?

MANUS I'm thinking, indeed, five golden sovereigns was a small enough thing, sir.

> SHANE *stares at* MANUS, *then at* SARAH, *then back to* MANUS.

SHANE Ah's ain't no black niggerman, Boss. Ah's just pu-ah white trash, Ah's just nuthin', suh, Ah's just nuthin' at all. (*Dances and sings*) 'Oh, dem golden sovereigns, Oh, dem golden sovereigns — '

MANUS *lifts the gun and points it at him.*

MANUS Silence!

SHANE I have no idea what you're talking about, Manus.

MANUS You came in here. And I made you welcome. And in return you robbed me, sir.

SHANE Robbed?

MANUS You stole my son.

SARAH I seen you — in the boathouse — you and Philly stripped — I seen you — I watched it all — with my own eyes — you and him, you dirty bastard — I seen it all — you dirty, dancing bastard!

SHANE She's hysterical.

SARAH I seen you! I seen you!

SHANE (*To* MANUS) For God's sake you don't heed her, do you?

SARAH (*To* MANUS) Ask him is it true? Ask him! Ask him!

SHANE *She* wanted to sleep with me.

SARAH With that thing, Manus! Is it the truth or is it a lie?

SHANE I wouldn't have her. That's what's eating her.

SARAH Deny it! Deny it! Deny it! Look at the face! Look at the slippery eyes! He can't! He can't! 'Cos I seen him! I seen him!

MANUS Is it the truth?

SHANE What? Is what the truth?

SARAH It is or it isn't? It is or it isn't?

SHANE Look at her for Christ's sake! She's insane!

SARAH It is or it isn't? Yes or no. Which is it?

SHANE I'll get Philly. He'll —

MANUS Back!

SARAH You've had enough with Philly, engineer. He robbed you, Manus. He robbed me. Shoot him! Shoot him!

SHANE Manus, please, Manus, listen, listen to me —

SARAH Shoot him! Shoot him!

SHANE Manus, I swear to God —

SARAH Shoot him!

MANUS *brings the gun up.* SHANE *crouches before him.*

SHANE Manus, Manus, Manus, please, please, Manus, please, please.
SARAH Shooooot!
MANUS I — I — I — I —
SARAH Give it to me! I'll kill the tramp.

She rushes to MANUS *and grabs the gun. In that moment* SHANE *bolts for the door.*

SHANE (*As he dashes away*) Peter! Save me, Peter! Save me!

He gets halfway across the street. SARAH *fires. He falls on his knees.*

Peter . . .

He falls on his face. SARAH *stares at him. All passion is gone. Her mouth is open. Her whole body limp. The gun drops from her hands. Very softly she begins to lament — an almost animal noise.*
Blackout.

ACT TWO

Scene Three

The beginning of dawn the following morning. MANUS *is huddled over a dead fire. He is mumbling inarticulately: but his voice is so modulated that we know he is talking to himself — posing questions and answering them. He rises from the fire and shuffles around the kitchen. He has aged a lot — the assurance has gone from his bearing. He goes to the door and looks out. With his hand he massages his chest and shoulders for heat. As he shuffles around he mumbles to himself.*

MANUS Where's my stick, Rosie? Rosie? Rosie — my stick! (*He finds it*) Why do you hide it on me? The baby? The baby? It's always the baby. I'll never get used to carrying this thing, woman; never. (*Suddenly he comes alert*) He's back, Sarah! He's back!

He goes out to the street to meet JOE *who enters left.*

Well?

JOE *walks briskly past him and goes into the kitchen.* MANUS *trots after him.*

Well, boy?

During the following conversation JOE *shaves busily.*

How is he?

JOE Ill.

MANUS I know he's ill. What happened? Where did you take him?

JOE To the Ballybeg hospital.

69

MANUS Well?

JOE They patched him up as best they could.

MANUS But he'll live?

JOE Maybe.

MANUS How bad is he?

JOE I thought he was for death in the boat. He came round a bit in the hospital.

MANUS He lost a power of blood. What did they say?

JOE Even if he lives he'll never walk again. His spine's shattered.

MANUS He's lying there in Ballybeg?

JOE They could do nothing for him. They sent him away in an ambulance.

MANUS Away? Away where to?

JOE Dublin. He wasn't fit to travel but he'd die if he was left there. He looked like a ghost lying on the stretcher. Still trying to act the clown though.

MANUS Did he say anything about the law?

JOE Who?

MANUS Peter. The engineer.

JOE No.

MANUS Didn't the doctor ask?

JOE He told them he was out after rabbits and tripped going across a ditch.

Pause.

MANUS It was a bad do. It was a sorry day Red Doherty brought them in among us.

JOE Was it you or her?

MANUS What?

JOE Shot him.

MANUS Her. When the time came I — I — I — (*He sits at the fire*) Their stuff's still below.

JOE Peter says throw it in the tide.

MANUS What are you shaving for?

JOE It's morning.

MANUS That's true. It's morning. And he'll never walk again.

JOE If he lives. You should go to bed for a while.

MANUS I'll wait 'till Philly gets back.

JOE To use the gun on him, too?

JOE goes into his bedroom. He returns with a case and an armful of clothes.

MANUS Philly had nothing to do with — What's that?
JOE What does it look like?
MANUS You're not thinking of leaving, are you?
JOE The thinking's done.
MANUS Put that away, boy. You're going no place.

He grabs JOE's arm. JOE stands rigid. The grip is relaxed. JOE begins to pack.

You're making a mistake, Joe. This is your home, this is where you belong. Don't go now. Wait a month. Wait a week. Wait 'till you know what you're at. You're all throughother. Wait 'till you're settled. You'll think different when your head's settled.

JOE closes the case.

What's going to happen to us? How are we going to manage? You don't give a curse, do you? It doesn't matter to you that your father's handicapped, does it? Not as long as you're taking care of yourself. That's all you ever thought of — yourself. Go ahead. Go ahead. Think of yourself. You owe me nothing, nothing at all. I deserve no better — me that lost a limb away slaving for you. Go ahead. Clear out. I'll not starve. I can always scrape a hole and grow enough spuds to fill me.

JOE Come with me if you want.
MANUS You're going to London! To Anna! You're going to marry her. That's it. You're going to marry her and come back and raise your family here. That's it, man, that's it.

He goes to the mantelpiece, opens the envelope, thrusts the money at JOE.

71

Here you are — money and all. And you'll live here, in
this house, this house'll be yours and the upper field
and the far bog and the two boats — all yours — and
this is where your family'll grow up — here — their
grandfather's, their great-grandfather's house.

JOE   I'm not taking that.

MANUS   You'll need it, man. You'll need it and more.

He produces more notes from his pocket.

That's not near enough. Here — here — you'll need
that, too — your fare over and back — a wedding —
digs — new clothes. Here — take it all. What use have
I for it? Take it all.

JOE *lifts one note.*

JOE   That'll pay my way to Glasgow.

MANUS   Glasgow? She's in London!

JOE   I'm going to Glasgow. To Bosco and the boys.

JOE *takes the letter, the proposal, tears it up, and tosses
it into the fire.*

MANUS   And what about Anna Con? What about the wedding?

JOE *goes into his bedroom.*

(*Shouts*) It's them — them queers! I should have killed
the two of them when I had them! What we had wasn't
much but what there was was decent and wholesome!
And they blighted us! They cankered us! They
blackened the bud that was beginning to grow again!
My curse on them! My curse of hell on the two of them!
Agus marbhfháisc orthu — an early shroud on them!

SARAH *enters from her bedroom. She is dressed in the
clothes she was wearing yesterday evening. Because of
the morning cold she has a shawl thrown over her
shoulders. She does not look at* MANUS. *She shuffles*

around the kitchen listlessly.

You didn't kill him.

SARAH I know.

MANUS All you did was maim him.

SARAH I heard.

MANUS If I had my two hands that wouldn't have been the story. And now he's going.

SARAH So.

MANUS Not to London — to Glasgow — to link up with the hooligans.

SARAH He'll have a bit of life there.

MANUS Life? What life is there working another man's land for a handful of money? What life is it fifteen men living and sleeping in a hovel no bigger than this kitchen?

SARAH He'll find out for himself. Maybe that's the thing'll please him.

MANUS A man that never saw a town bigger than Ballybeg.

SARAH I never seen anything as lovely as the Isle of Man. That'll do me. Many's the one lives and dies and doesn't see even that.

JOE enters ready for departure.

JOE I'm off to Scotland, Sarah.

SARAH You're right, too.

JOE Bosco'll write for me, let you know where I am, what's happening. Tell Philly I'll leave the boat tied up at the harbour out.

SARAH Goodbye, Joe.

He goes to MANUS who has turned away.

JOE I'm away, Father. (*Pause*) Father.

MANUS does not turn. JOE goes to the door, remembers the key in his pocket, stops.

(*To SARAH*) Anna's key. Maybe you'd light an odd . . . No. Let the fieldmice look after themselves.

He tosses the key on the table and leaves. SARAH *follows him out to the street.*

SARAH Good luck, Joe. Good luck.
JOE Good luck, amen.

Pause. MANUS *goes to the door and watches his son leave.*

MANUS Not a bad lump of a man. He'll not go under. (*Pause*) All the same there isn't the same tidiness about him as there is about Philly. (*Pause*) Philly'll miss him. Man but Philly'll miss him.
SARAH He'll get over it.

MANUS *joins her on the street.*

MANUS Will you do something for me, Sarah?
SARAH What?
MANUS Don't tell him about what happened here last night. The sooner it's forgotten the better. Will you do that for me?

She shrugs indifferently.

And sure maybe Joe was right. Maybe they only went into the boathouse to change their clothes because they were wet.
SARAH They didn't have a change of clothes.
MANUS Maybe so. Maybe so. But it's that dark in yon place you could imagine anything. One night when I went into it there was a sail hanging from the roof and as sure as God I thought it was a sheep making for me. I could have sworn it was a sheep making for me . . . it's that dark in yon place you could imagine anything. Maybe you . . .

SARAH *has walked off left. He goes into the kitchen, looks around aimlessly, picks up the shaving things* JOE *left behind.* PHILLY *enters right. He leaves the outboard at the door and enters the kitchen.*

You're early back.

PHILLY Aye.

MANUS I didn't expect you for a while yet. Was it no good?

PHILLY It wasn't much.

MANUS How many?

PHILLY Seven.

MANUS Seven? Well. That itself. Even seven. It's this damned weather. Going to destroy everything.

He gets a notebook and writes in the latest score.

Seven and two's nine . . . that makes two hundred and nine so far. With a bit of luck you could still tip the thousand before the season ends. No trouble with the engine?

PHILLY No. But I think I split the keel on the rocks coming in. I'll have to haul her up and have a look at her. Is Joe up yet?

MANUS I'll help you. I can do it.

PHILLY Joe and me'll manage.

MANUS Joe's away out.

PHILLY What for?

MANUS Joe's away altogether.

PHILLY Gone?

MANUS To Glasgow.

PHILLY *laughs heartily.*

PHILLY The bold Joe! Well that's a good one! I thought he'd never try it!

MANUS To Bosco and the boys.

PHILLY That's the best yet. Joe's left the nest, eh? Man he'll break his heart to be away from home. It must have been a sudden notion?

MANUS You wouldn't know with that fella. Maybe he had it all planned before the others pulled out.

PHILLY Last night?

MANUS This morning. The strangers went with him.

PHILLY They're away?

MANUS When they got the chance of the boat out.

PHILLY Their stuff's still there. I seen it coming in.

MANUS They left in a hurry. Joe — you know Joe — he was fussing and complaining about missing the Derry bus — wouldn't give them time to pack right. Damn little they had anyway apart from what they stood up in.

PHILLY There's the tent and the gear inside.

MANUS They're gone anyway.

PHILLY And Joe! God, that's a good one! (*Laughs*) Himself and the boys'll do some damage in Glasgow when they get going.

MANUS I think I'll go and lie down for a while. I didn't sleep too well last night.

SARAH *comes in with an armful of turf.*

PHILLY He tells me the young brother's away!

SARAH So.

PHILLY The best I've heard yet. Whoever he works to is getting a real bull. Not that he'll stick it long.

SARAH He'll stick it.

PHILLY Joe? Three weeks'll do him and he'll come creeping back. Joe couldn't live anywhere but here. I know Joe. And the strangers are gone, too. A real red-out.

SARAH Will you eat now or will you sleep first?

PHILLY I'll eat.

MANUS Give me a call in an hour.

PHILLY Father.

MANUS *stops at the bedroom door.*

Hadn't they a wee cooker below in the tent, a yoke that worked on paraffin oil?

MANUS They had.

PHILLY I'll go down and fetch it. A right handy wee gadget that. Useful in the morning when the fire's not lit.

MANUS I don't want it. I couldn't work it .

PHILLY There's nothing to it. Strike a match and away it goes. And the tent — the best of good canvas that. Put that

over a haystack and it would be as dry as snuff.
MANUS It wouldn't be healthy.
PHILLY Healthy? Sure you wouldn't see a haystack out that hasn't a covering. What d'you want to do? Let the stuff lie there 'till the next high tide takes it? I doubt you're getting old!

MANUS *goes into his bedroom.*

Healthy! What's wrong with him?

SARAH *kneels at his feet and pulls off his thighboots.*

SARAH How was the salmon?
PHILLY Bad.
SARAH He's keeping a score in a wee notebook.
PHILLY I seen him.

Pause.

SARAH You'll never make £200 now.
PHILLY It might pick up.
SARAH That means you're stuck for another year.
PHILLY Maybe.

Pause.

The place'll be quiet without Joe thumping about. But he'll be back. I'll give him three weeks.
SARAH We'll get used to it.
PHILLY The wonder is he made the mainland even.

Fade to black.